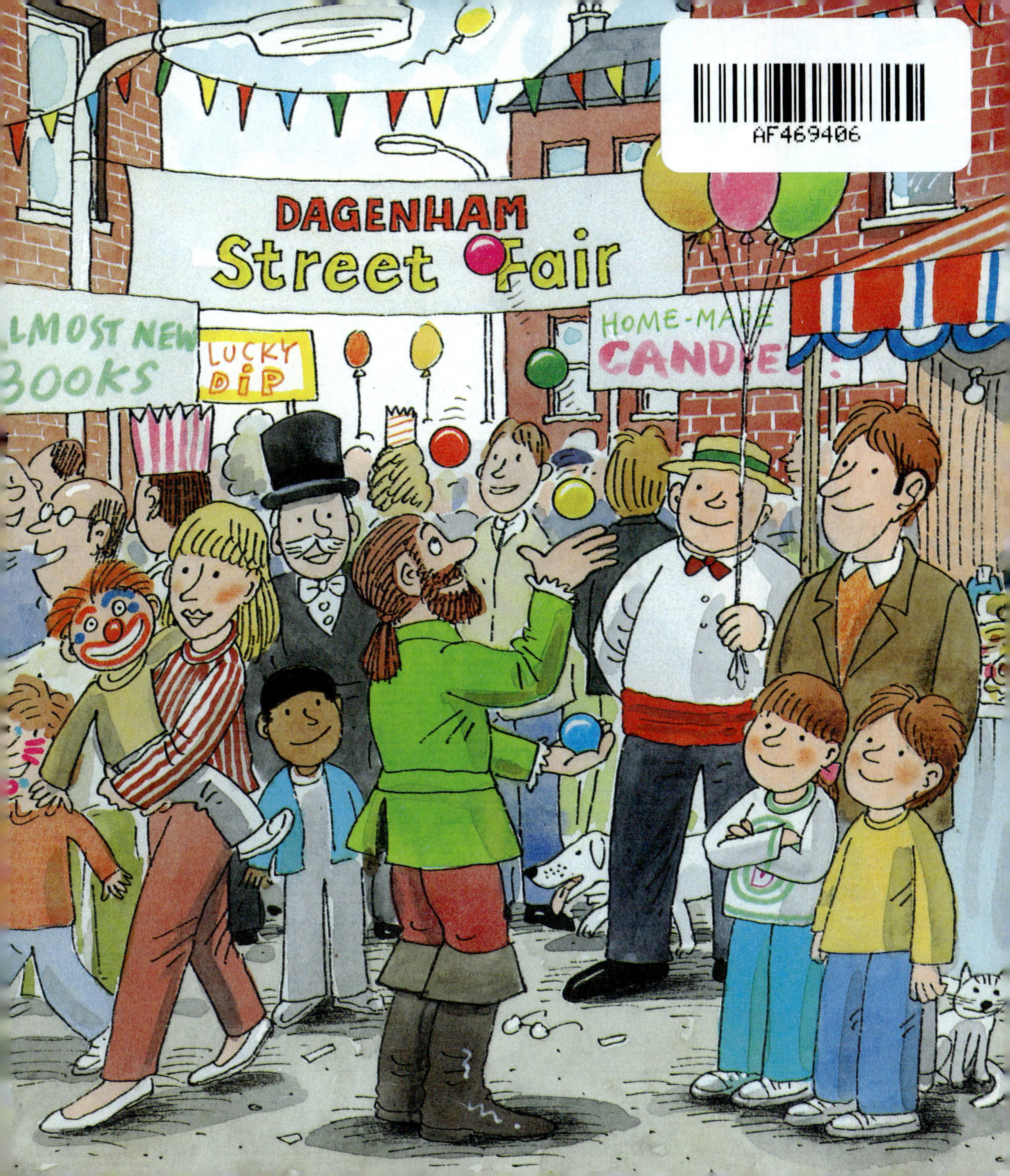
DAGENHAM
Street Fair
LUCKY DIP
HOME-MADE

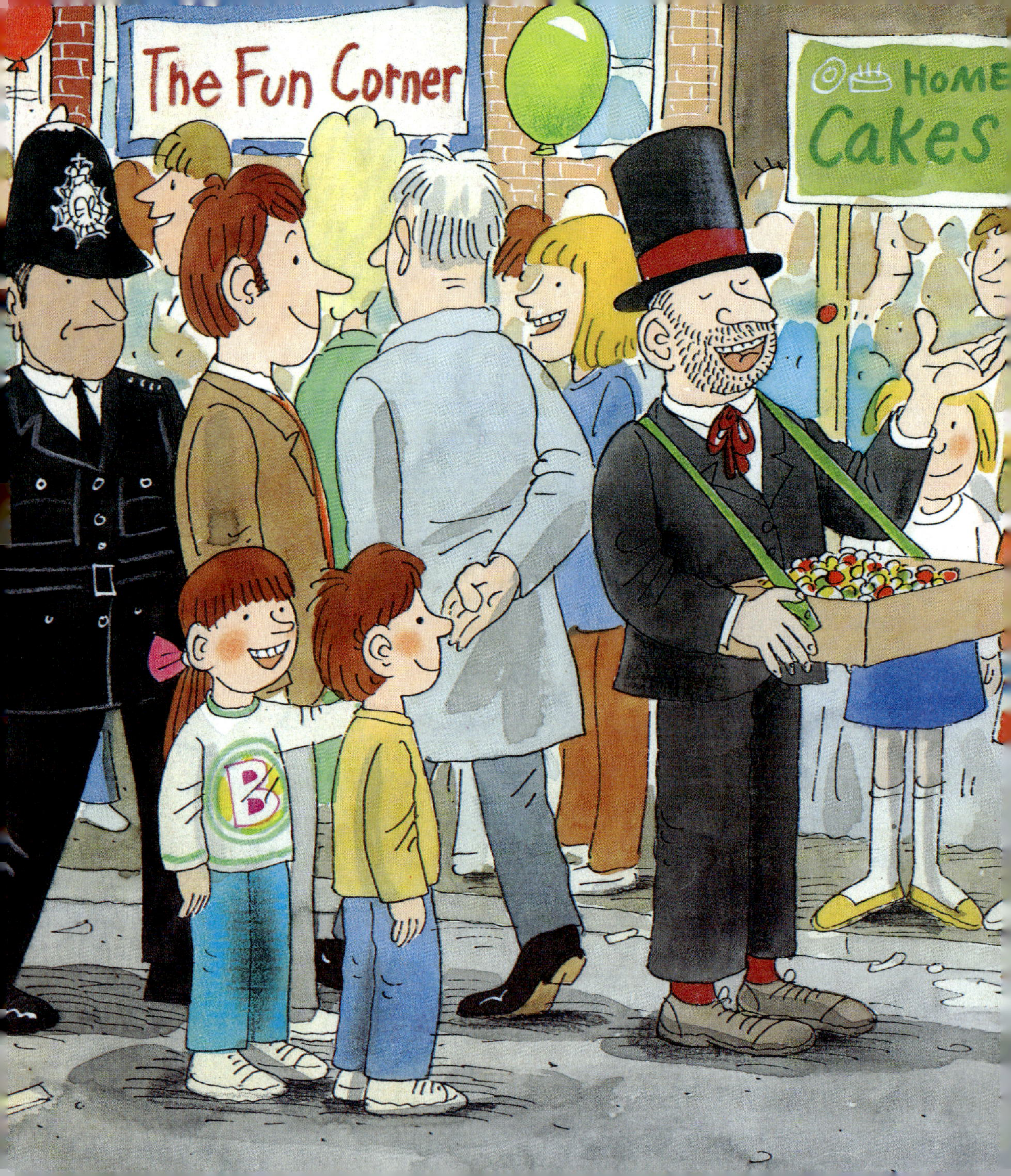
The Fun Corner
HOME
Cakes
B

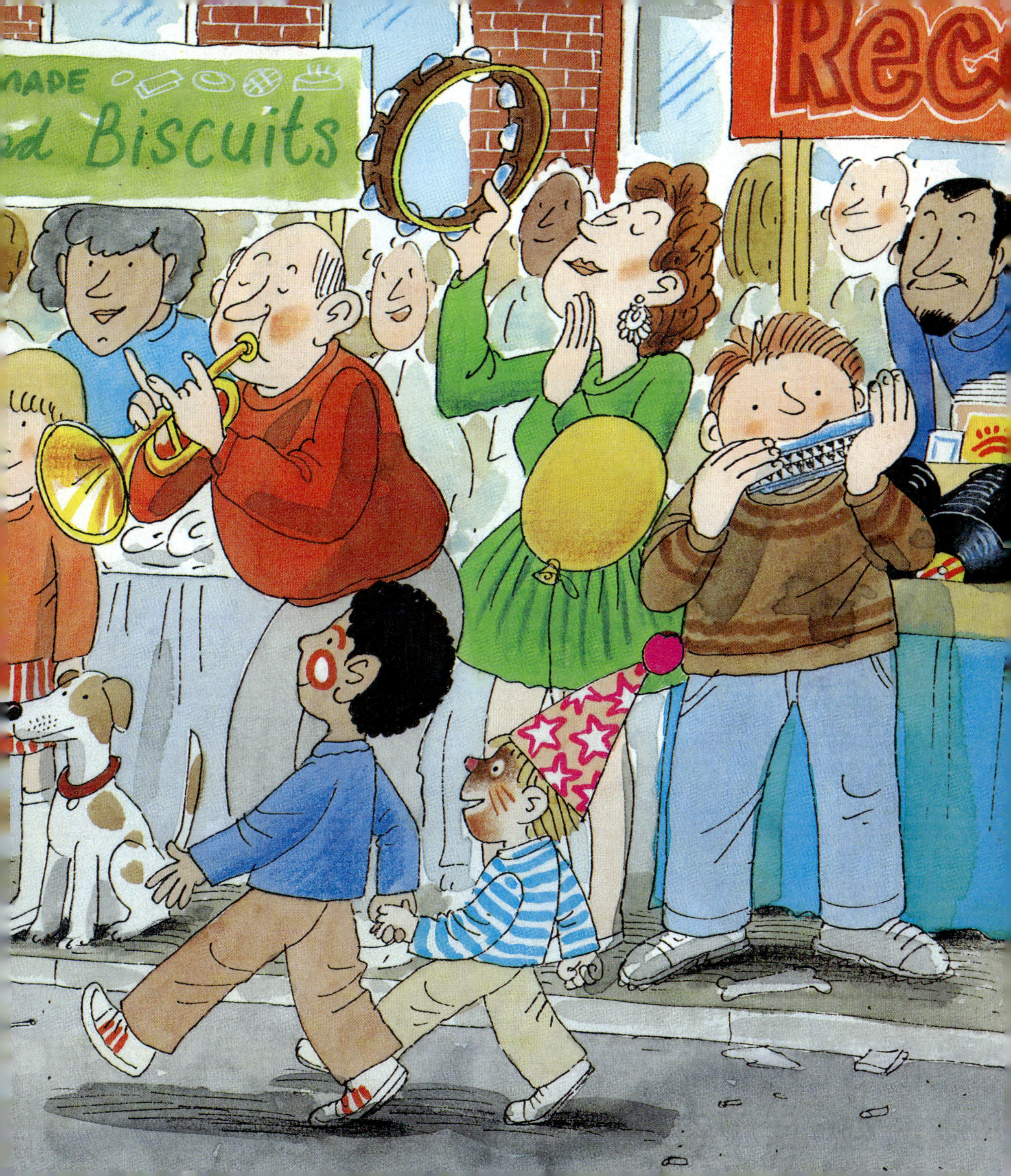
MADE
Biscuits

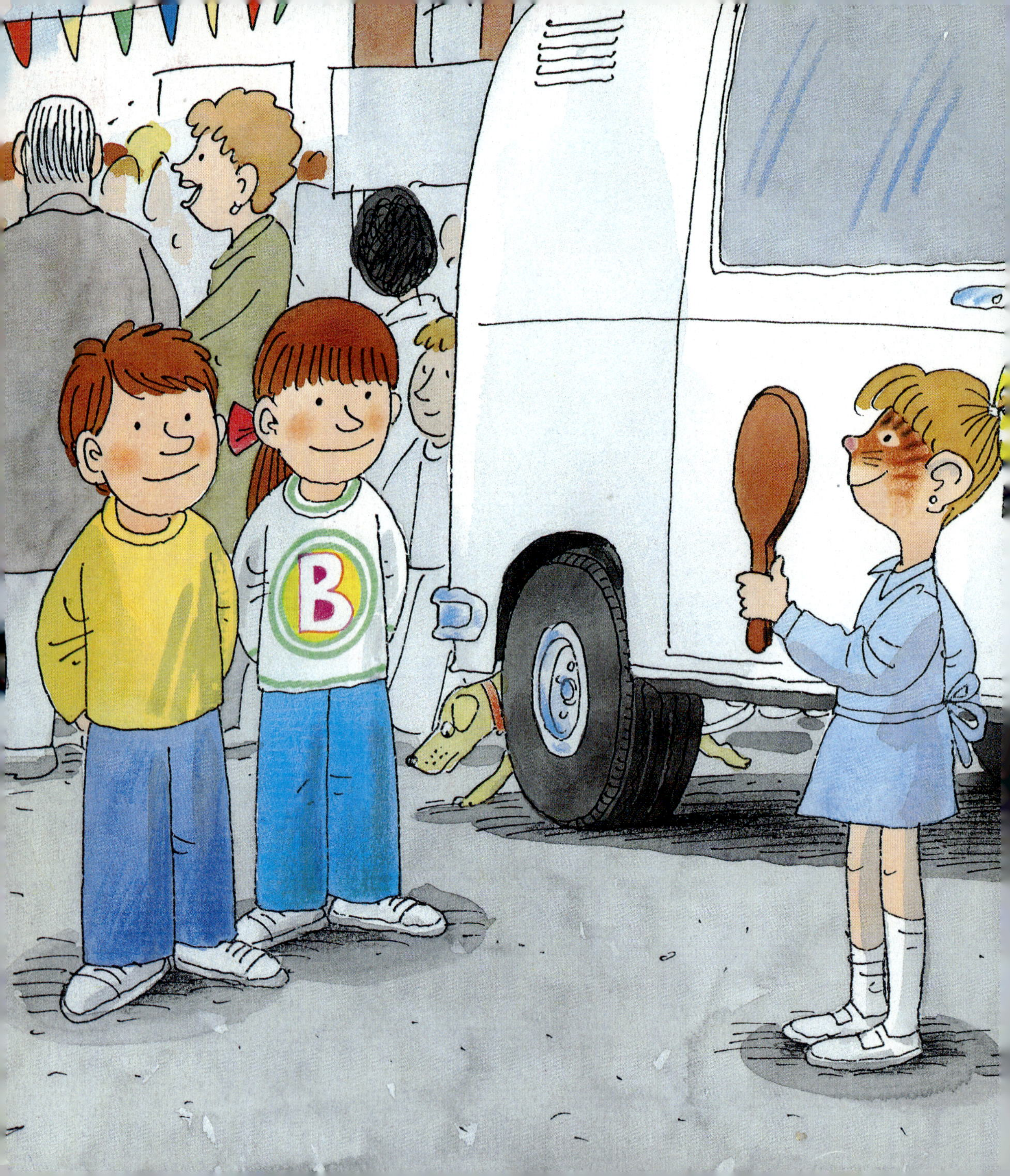

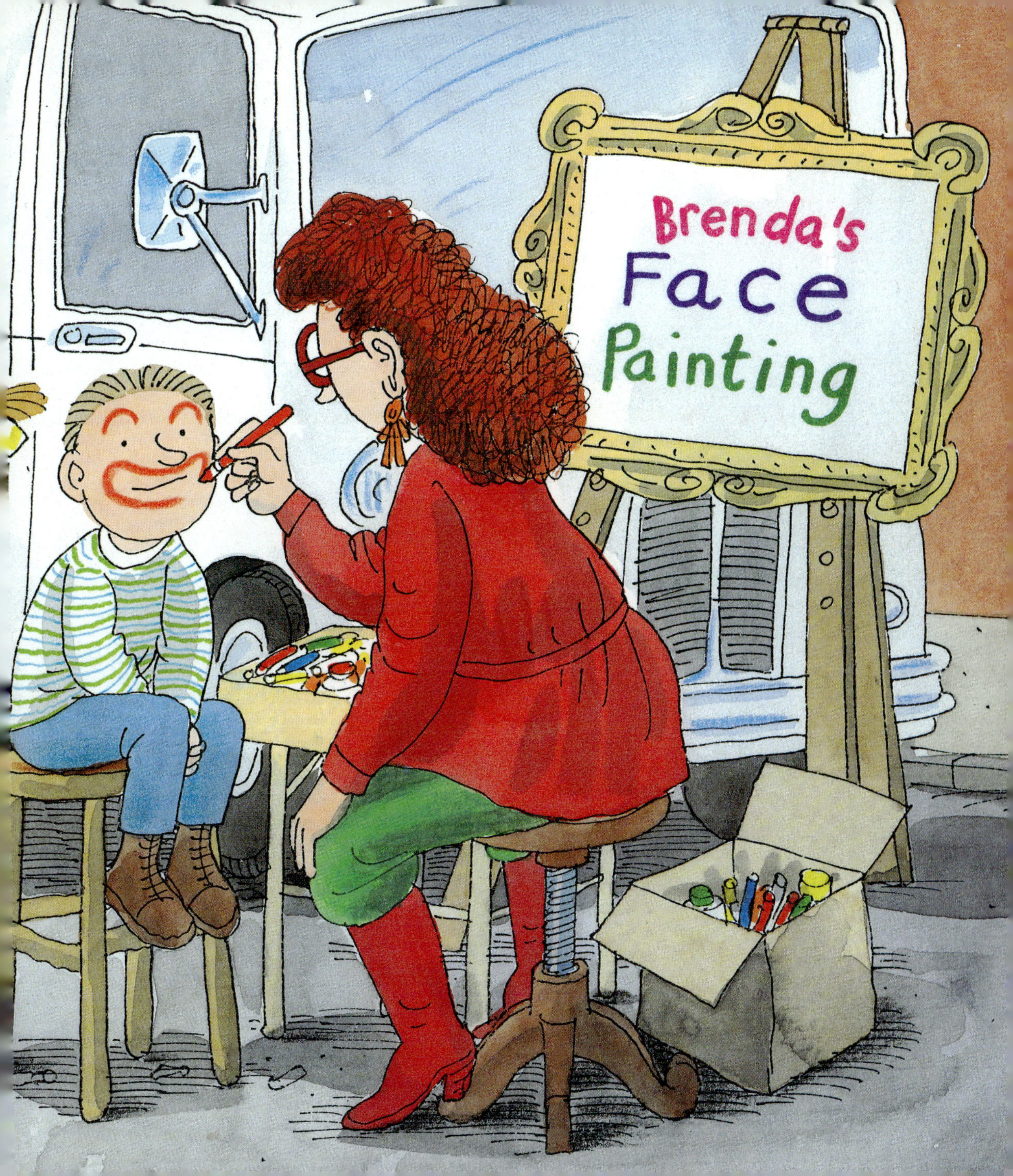
Brenda's
Face
Painting

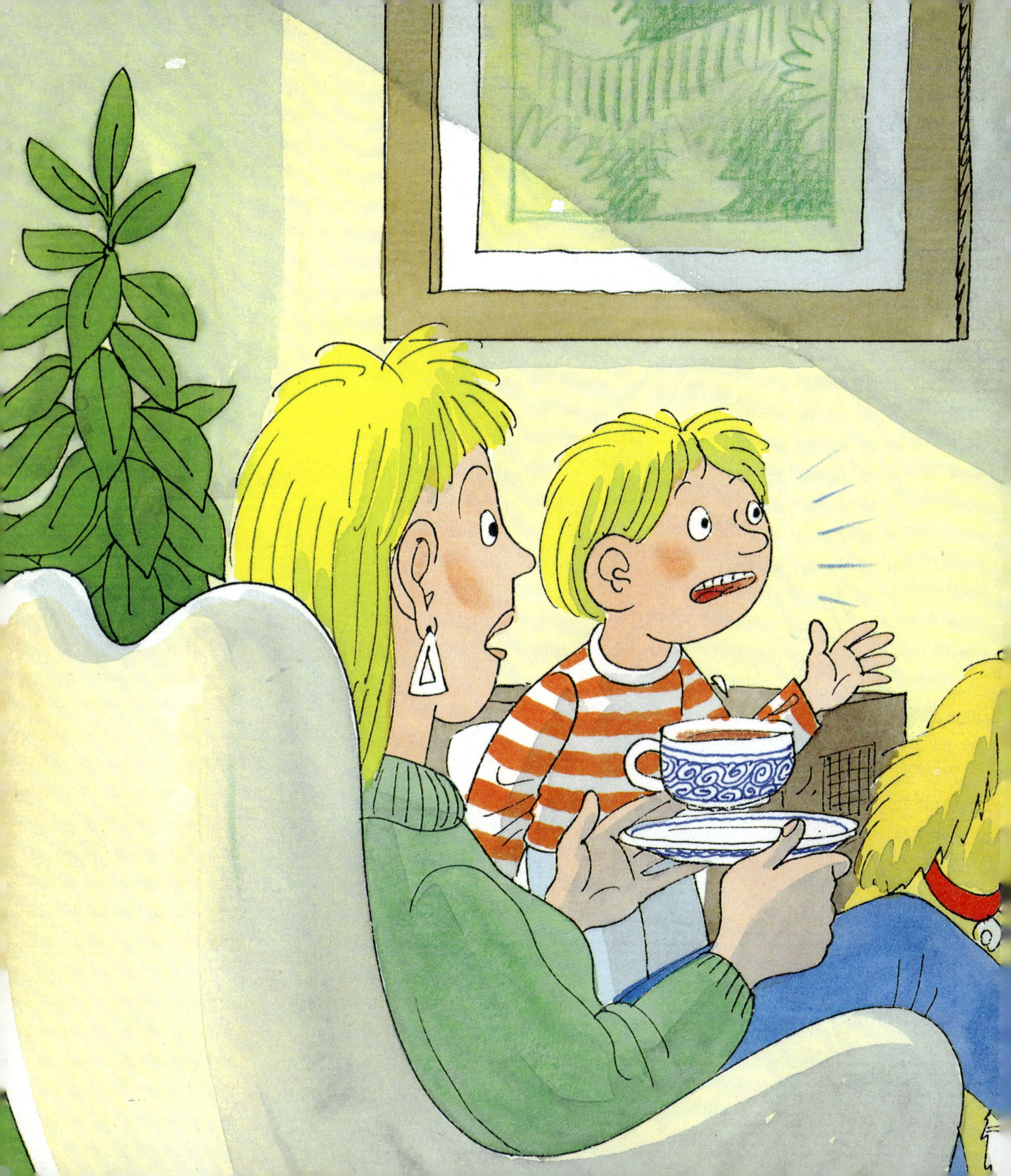

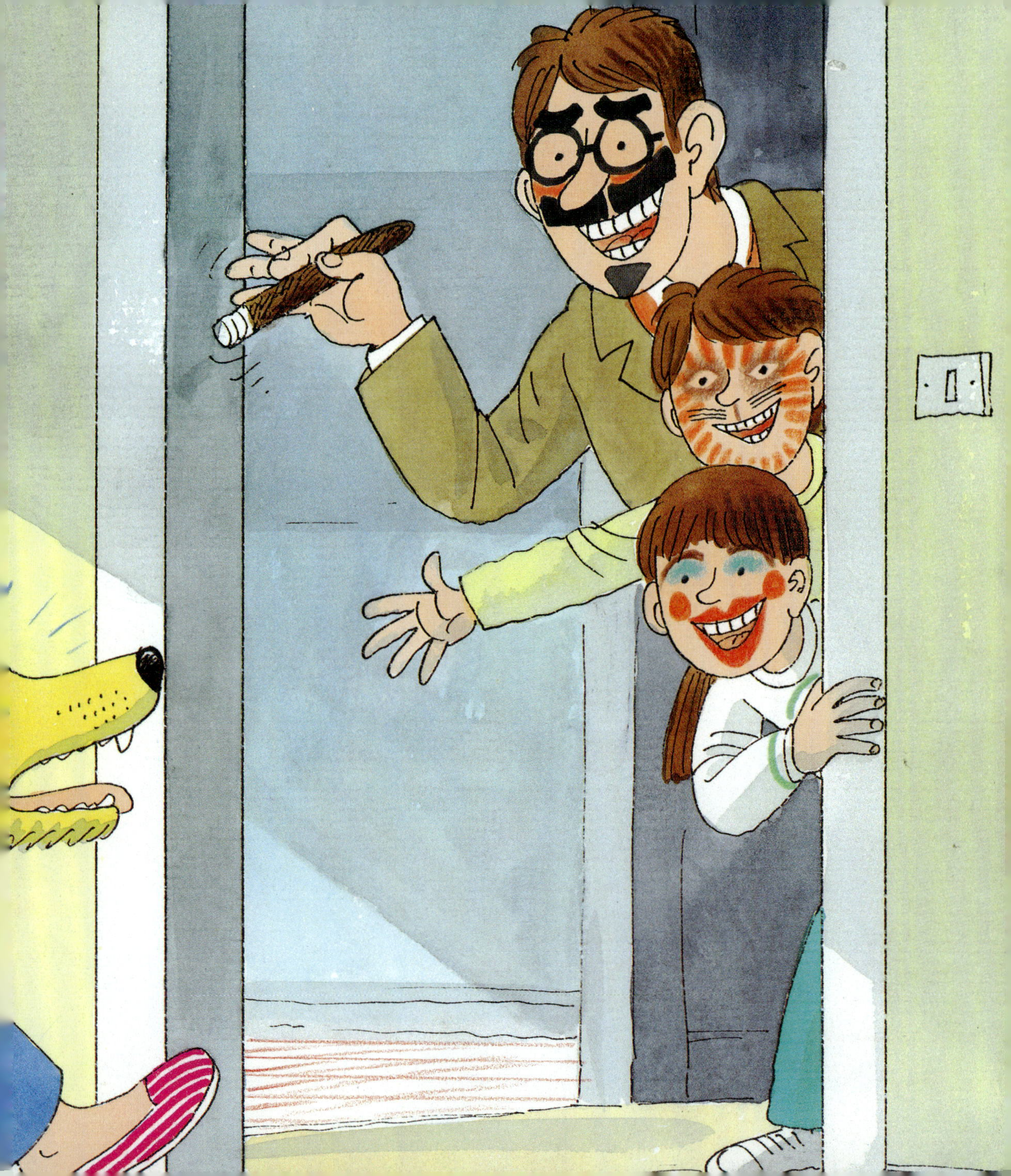

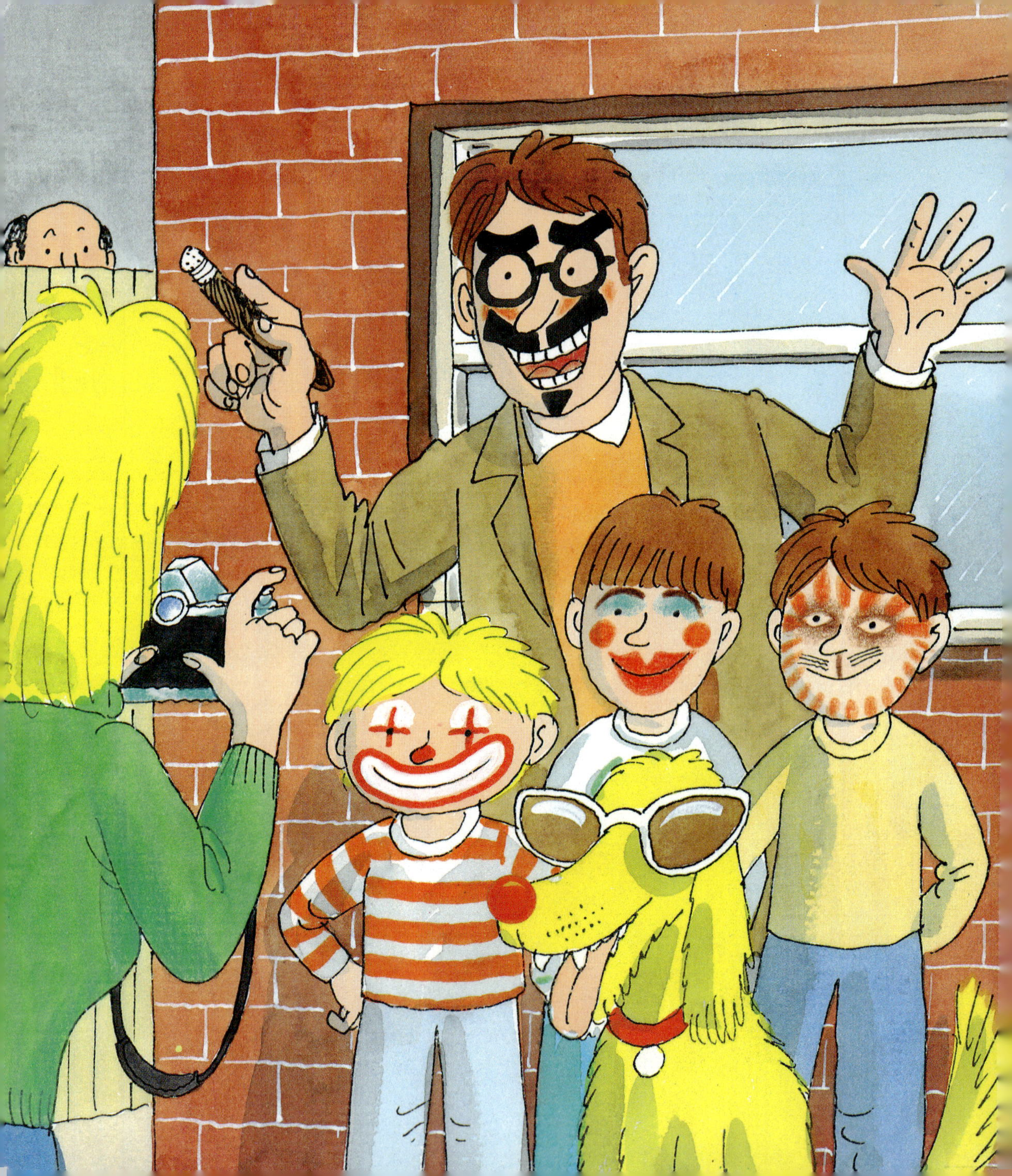